I0538412

BareBackMagazine

March 2014

This is a work of fiction. The characters, incidents, and dialogue are the products of the authors' imaginations and are not to be construed as real. Any resemblance to actual events or person, living or dead, is entirely coincidental.

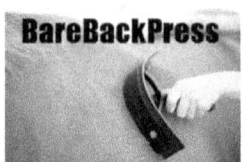

BareBackPress
Hamilton, Ontario, Canada
For enquires visit www.barebackpress.com
For information contact press@barebacklit.com

Editors Peter Jelen and Damon Ferrell Marbut.
Copy Editor Mike Algera.
Cover layout and art: "In the Heart of the City" © 2014 Peter Jelen.
Portions have appeared in The Writer's Block, Issue 6, July, 2010, *Referential Magazine*, October, 2010, and *Cache Magazine*, July, 2008

POETRY

FICTION

FLASH FICTION

POETRY

Okay, I'll Stay For Dinner. But Only If You Have Chocolate Vegan Cheesecake For Dessert
Laura Stamps

When I step through the door of his
condo, chilly air bathes my face,
a welcome relief from the humid
heat of the day. "Would you like
something to drink?" he asks.
"Water is fine," I say. I set my bag
of cat remedies on the kitchen counter,
which is the wildest thing I've ever
seen. It looks like an artist painted
a colorful abstract across his counter-
tops and then sealed the paint with
gloss varnish. "Where is this stray
kitten you told me about?" I ask.
Before he can reply, a black furball
darts out from beneath the sofa.
"There you are," I say, scooping
the frisky kitten into my arms. It
clings to me, its purr loud, graveled.
"Interesting," he says. "Usually it
runs away from visitors, not to them."
I smile and kiss the silken top of the
kitten's head. "I have a way with
cats," I say. He drops several ice
cubes into two glasses and fills them
with spring water. "I can see that,"
he says. I fluff the kitten's thick fur
and stroke its paws. They're huge.
"I was right," I say. "This is a Maine
Coon." I set the kitten on the kitchen
table and lift its tail. "A female,"
I say. Cupping her tiny face in my
hands, I study her crusty eyes.
"She's got an eye infection," I say,
"but that's typical for most strays
and easy to heal." I reach into
my bag for a bottle of goldenseal.
Emptying one capsule of the
medicinal herb into a cup of warm
water, I show him how to strain it
through a paper towel into another
cup. Then I bathe the kitten's eyes
in the goldenseal tea, using a cotton
ball. The solution is so soothing
the kitten stops struggling, her purr

louder than ever. He frowns, far
from convinced. "You may have to
come over here and do this for me
every day," he says. "I doubt she
or I will survive it if I try." I set the
wiggling kitten on the floor. "You'd
be surprised," I say. He crumples
part of a paper towel into a ball and
tosses it over the kitten's head. She
leaps after it and bats it under the sofa.
"Stay for dinner," he says, when he
hands me a glass of water. "Please.
I'd like that."

About the Author:

Laura Stamps is a Pagan novelist and poet living in South Carolina. Her work has
been nominated for seven Pushcarts and published by Texas Review Press, Ninety-
Six Press, and McGraw-Hill, among others. She enjoys creating experimental forms
for her prose poems, blurring the line between fiction and poetry. You can find her
every day at Tumblr. She's addicted to it. Really. She is.

Strangers
Poppy Scarlett

She painted them sombre
colourlessly dressed – far out of attainment.
She never did name them.
In her obscurity was where they belonged.
So different, that man, and that woman
as if knowing, the world was already too heavy an obligation
deposited in its prehistoric
ochre lichen, covered mountains
with a child, already in residence.
Always that faint
nauseating fear of falling – saved only
by a small flock of passing gods.
Who would then, move her on, like some long
lost weary traveler -
in the hope, that someone soon, would come forward
and make the ultimate claim?

About the Author:

Poppy lives in Cumbria - a stunning rural part of the UK - famed for the Lake District known to many holiday makers worldwide. These days, there is just Poppy and her animals to look after - leaving more time for writing. Most of her work is based on real life, either her own - or from experiences that have happened to good friends and family.

If you are left
Tony McCafferty

If you are left when I should die,
then for a time tears will fall free.
But know that I would wish that you
could smile when you remember me.

No eulogy chiselled in stone,
or marble monument to name
a simple man who lived his life;
who never sought the pride in fame.

Within the grounds of Ratby Church
there is a plot created where
ashes decay, but are unmarked,
and I'd like mine to join them there.

There is a seat where you might rest
and think awhile of all we had.
The greatest of the gifts, I think,
was being known as Mum and Dad.

And if one day upon the seat
someone should gently take your hand,
please know, if I could be aware,
I would, with pleasure, understand.

About the Author:

Tony McCafferty lives in retirement with his wife in a small village in central England. He is a Great Grandfather who enjoys spending time with his family. He has had a varied working life which has included 22 years in the Military and 10 years as a College Lecturer. These days he likes to write poetry as a relaxing hobby. His work has appeared in an earlier edition of Bareback Magazine (August 2013) and he has won prizes for his poetry in village competitions.

(3) poems
Sherry Steiner

crescent
lace
buttoned tight;
fully
clothed velvets
brass knobs –
a walking stick
on
the side;
butlered variances
short stop mishaps;
finally
irish rum
served
upright
in albania
in 1903;
that is.

---

unfamiliar
protocol bellies
the beached whale;
monogrammed
in season –
strolling at water's edge
festering broadband
attention
to a mug of java;
honey spoonfuls
lilac pleasures
brilliant
inconsistencies.

---

branching
figurative absurdities in
a delicate
configuration;
meeting agenda foiled.
rolled in a serrated box
cast your vote.
draped in political canopies
bach plays on

as
history furiously
pedals
between
the lines.

About the Author:
Sherry Steiner: lives in Housatonic MA, originally from NYC. Published writer of off-beat poetry, monologues, flash fiction and musical performance pieces, arts educator, exhibiting visual artist and more. For detailed background information: www.sherrysteiner.com.

Closing Time
(For the recent victims of the textile industry)
Blaithin Allain

Warehouse remnants,
Purple embers of a neon in cinders,
Walls like skeletons spindle a sewing factory
As moon drifts on blue-dust shadows
Blows the eerie lime alive,
Wind ruminating rumours of buried workers
Cremated in secret cellars

By the dumped machines,
Wheels spin seams of redundancy ;
Unseen fingers numbly sewing
Baby buttons to hung puppets

Beneath the dummies, a stack of arms
Nakedly air, stretch, stir
Their faces, erased of features ;
Invisible figures join the limbs,
Dress the dolls in eyeless laces,
Bead embroideries to wasted members,
Stitching lips to puckered traces
And dangle-dance their thimbles,
Depository of tiny threads
Round the ruins of cranes,
Pitching wreckage cables,
Like carnivals for jumble sale
Where puppets played the patrons game,
Where puppeteers have tossed their twine
And whispering now the seamstress dies
As costumes flop to moonlit shrouds
The clocks have stopped
It's closing time.

About the Author:

Blaithin Allain lives in Brittany France. She is currently resident artist at Morlaix Theatre. Her poetry has been published in France by the CRBC (University Review, Department of Celtic Studies). She has had poems published by The Boyne Berries Magazine in Ireland and by Pulsar magazine and Unquiet Desperation in the UK. She is currently working on a play which will include poetry and elements of Celtic mythology. She is married and has two teenage Kids.

Arctic Tourist: Final Song
Lesley Strutt

I'm looking for…I don't know what I'm looking for*.

I name the north in bird and beast:
Ivory, Polar, Gyre
Kittiwake, Kittiwake, Kittiwake.

The north sends back its name:
World-uyunga.

It harpoons me – ice and rock and pink sky.
I am caught on its string.

When my crying stops
it makes a purse of me.
Places in me one pebble. Names it

Lisli-uyunga.

Shadow-licked
glacier tongued

I am looking.

About the Author:
Lesley Strutt's ancestral roots are Irish and she is a descendant of the Bard of Bytown - William Pitman Lett. Her poetry plays lightly with the lived human experience, essence, and love in all its guises. Her poems have been published by Leaf Press, Bywords, The Literary Review and the Canadian Woman Studies Journal and included in anthologies edited by Patrick Lane.

Wintry
Osvaldo Rocha

Nothing to us became the shadow-shaped birches
along the lonely long occurrence of winter.
Nothing went fine, we were the leaves
we had cuddled, but it was our first winter
under the tin trees.
Nebula stuck on a woody pane,
we are moisture, we are wool and skin
and sometimes disgrace.

Weary is the walk that leads the lambs
into the newly lambed stream
when the salty rain bites on empty bowels,
as you have decided to yourself
(without pondering) what I must not deserve.
What I have been is what I will be, that is your hope,
and what I have said is the stain where I shall fade.
Wintry woodland in which my air was torn,
it is too late for the lambs, too late for your woes
and your fire-shaded distancing at night.

About the Author:
Osvaldo Rocha is a Mexican poet and translator of German and Scandinavian literature. His poems and translations appear in some Mexican journals as well as in *Tipton Poetry Journal *(USA), * Softblow *(Singapore), *Pericvlvm *(Spain-Iceland), *Amsterdam Sur* (Netherlands), * Cinosargo *(Chile), and elsewhere. He earned an MA in Old Norse at the University of Iceland and currently works as a lecturer in Guadalajara, Mexico.

Love Is
Kristal Lee Morningstarr

Broken hearts and bloody tears
is why we all lose ourselves;
love is sick, love is blind
love drives you to insanity.
Everyone I've ever loved has broken
my heart at least once,
I guess that's why I've broken the hearts
of all those I love at least twice.

About the Author:

To Kristal Lee Morningstarr, writing is like breathing; its second nature. When she was 19, she decided it's what she wanted to spend her life doing. Kristal is a member of the Ontario Poetry Society, and recently received Honourable Mention for "Love Is", in their Ultra Short Poem contest. She has also been published in three of their anthologies, "The Ultra Best Short Verse", "Spirit Eyes and Fire Flies" and also "Ropedancer.

Cancelled
Michael E. Stone

Cancelled – a stamp
with black ink showing date,
place, sometimes country

Cancelled — a flight
to somewhere
some town, some land.

Cancelled — a meeting
that might
have changed my life.

Cancelled – a page
in life's book,
replaced by another.

Cancelled — a check
overdrawn on life's
bank.

Cancelled. Cancelled.

The End.

About the Author:
Michael Stone was born in England in 1938. His family moved to Australia in 1941, where he received his schooling, up to the completion of his BA (Hons.) degree in 1960. He lives in Jerusalem with his family. He has published poems in numerous literary journals as well as translations of medieval Armenian poetry. His poetry has also been anthologized in a number of collections. He is now retired.

FICTION

Henry And The Sun
Chris Milam

Jasmine DuPont. Lacrosse player, editor of the school paper The Hillsboro Chronicle, debutante, amateur photographer, slayer of hearts and the object of my desire. Jasmine DuPont. Pale-blue eyes that danced in their sockets, mahogany-colored hair tied in a simple ponytail, tanned and flawless skin that shimmered. Her typical uniform were snug but not too snug jeans, t-shirts with quotes like "Carpe Diem" and "Dont Worry Be Happy." She always wore flip-flops that showed off her perfectly sculpted, lime-green tipped feet. Everybody lusted after her. The potheads, the ball players, the geeks, the prudes, the janitor, the professors, the activists, the lab rats and me. We all saw the grace in her walk and the wit in her talk and it was intoxicating. She was the Sun.

I sat on my porch sipping a caramel macchioto and chain-smoking Marlboro light 100s. I watched my neighborhood come to life. Kids playing wiffle ball, dads washing cars, moms pruning flowers, teens plotting their escape.

"Hey Henry, hot one today, ain't it"?

Barry. Always Barry with a comment about the weather or the Bengals or his wife's amazing tuna casserole.

"Its July, Barry, logic dictates it would be warm today"

"Yeah, Yeah, well, gotta finish mowing before the ole lady barks at me"

Fuck you Barry came out as "see ya"

I go back inside my house to escape further encroachment of my personal space. I wasn't a people person. Books, music and porn were all I needed. People thought I was a nice but quiet guy, intelligent and aloof. I said the right things and wore proper clothes, kept my lawn immaculate, took my trash to the curb on Monday nights, recycled, engaged the Barry's of the world when necessary but it was just a role I played. I was hiding in plain sight, the wolf drinking his coffee. The leopard with a weed-eater and a glass of lemonade. A chameleon.

I sit on my sofa, put some Lamontagne on the iPod and crack open my laptop. Check the local newspaper site for any breaking news, nothing. Check Facebook. Wanda the soccer mom from two houses down posting about God again. I guess the big guy overlooks her fucking Merle, the married truck driver with a tree trunk down his pants.

I go into my gallery of pictures. Mom drinking a Budweiser while cooking, Mom drinking a Budweiser while laughing, Mom taking a nap with a Budweiser sitting suspiciously on the end table. Mom liked beer and mom liked men. Mom didn't really like being a mom, though.

There's my dad with a book in his lap, his perfectly bearded face leering at the camera. He grew tired of Mom's daily dance with Mr Budweiser and her frequent excursions to a seedy motel with any guy that gave her a compliment. He took off for the gulf coast years ago. Married a sober hair stylist, popped out a couple more kids and joined a softball team. His American dream, minus me. His love for me comes in the form of a check made out to my landlord. I go to college, he pays my rent and we both skip the tender moments. As long as that check keeps coming, he'll always be Daddy to me.

I shut the laptop, grab a Harpoon IPA, light a smoke and go back in time.

Early May, The Commons were bustling with people. Lunchtime on campus for me wasn't about shoving pizza down my throat or socializing. I came to observe. I picked a spot in the northern corner that had the best sight lines and an enormous sycamore tree to shade me, not from the hammer of the mid day sun but from the other students. I sat down at a picnic table. Apparently, one benefit of paying a crippling tuition were these beautifully lacquered Oak tables. They would make Jesus the carpenter proud. Professor Morton with his cherry red Hummer and a penchant for young journalists probably benefitted from the tuition as well.

My Sun sat down at one of those majestic tables. Solo. I stared at her through my Ray Ban's, every perverts favorite tool of the trade. She had the look of a blue-blood, the air of a coddled princess. She sat with her back perfectly erect, her hair not even moving in the breeze. As if mother nature stood in awe of Jasmine's beauty and directed the wind at the fat girls with bad complexions and Twinkie cream on their fingers sitting nearby.

"My main man, Henry, what's up little buddy?"

Dear God. Phillip Denton. Smart kid with a loud mouth. Wearing his typical rugby shirt, khakis and sandals. He saves whales or feeds the poor or something. A volunteer kinda guy.

"Enjoying my solitude, Phil"

"You and your quiet introspection, I like it, man. Serenity and all that jazz, good for the soul"

"Something like that. What can I do for you, Phil?"

"Nothing, nothing at all. Just shooting the breeze, Henry. I hear Tabitha from Calculus class is keen on you. She likes the silent rogue types. You could do worse, Henry"

Tabitha Wood. No fashion sense, flat-chested, reads Twilight, laughs like a malnourished bovine, drinks wine coolers. Poems will never be written about her.

"I'll pass"

"You're too selective, dude. A guys gotta get laid occasionally. You're not putting a ring on her, H-bomb"

I was not swayed. Guys wanted one of two things: fuck a girl or find a girl with a good soul. That's it. A good soul, that cracks me up. If you're looking for that, just stop by the trailer park on Lafayette Street. Lots of single moms with kind hearts and sweet souls live there. With three kids running around and no man at home and a beat-up vagina, you best have a nice disposition and be receptive to anal sex because you have nothing else to offer.

I wanted Jasmine. She would look good on my arm. Simple as that. Walk in a bar with her and people take notice. I'd be King dick for a night. Pretty girls that came from a privileged upbringing smelled different, like a fresh orchid, talked different, similar to a lady Shakespeare and cried different, tears of honey and wine. It appealed to me. I wanted a classy girl who could quote Flannery O'Connor or James Joyce, not Stephenie Meyer. I wanted a girl who was unblemished by tragedy or a low-income. Poor girls gave their pussy away for a cold beer or dinner at Red Lobster. Buy them some gas station roses and they give you an all-access card to their body, their panties hit the floor quicker than you can cough. I didn't picture Jasmine in that manner, it would take more than shrimp scampi and a Coors light to reveal her sweet mystery.

"Sorry, Phil but I've got a lot of shit on my mind right now"

"No prob. It's all good Henry. I've got to get down to the soup kitchen anyway. The homeless need to be fed and I love helping them. Later."

Yeah because what a homeless person truly needs is a bowl of vegetable soup not a place to live or anything. Dumb fuck.

"See ya" I forced out.

With Phil off saving the world, I could focus my gaze on My Sun once again. She had a tray of food in front of her and a bottle of Evian water. No RC cola for this gal. I decided to approach.

I put the ray bans in my pocket, I didn't want to come across as a pretentious douche and walked over to her table and sat down. Seriously, that table was crafted by a Viking or something, it belonged in a museum. She glanced up at me indifferently.

I wanted to ask her if I could watch her eat her tuna sandwich. I would enjoy that. Her slender fingers lightly gripping the bread as she slowly lifts it up to her sultry lips. Her mouth opening to reveal teeth as white as pure snow, her neck moving slightly forward as graceful as a swan, her eyes tasting the meal before she takes a delicate bite. It registered somewhere in my mind that I might creep her out with that question, so I played it safe.

"Hey Jasmine"

"Hey Henry"

"How is the paper coming along" I ask.

"Fine. Working on a story about Professor Morton"

"Wild guess, he's got an aspiring young journalist in his sights again?"

"Not in his sights, in his bed. He asked her to stop by his apartment Saturday night to supposedly go over an edit he was doing on her Syrian Refugee article. Strangely, he used a vintage Cabernet Sauvignon wine and veiled threats to clean up her paper. Oh and he abused his power and basically forced her to have sex so I'm taking him down. Tenured professors love the weight of the crown, I'm going knock it off his head"

"Good for you, Jasmine. Taking on authority is courageous, I admire that. Men abusing women, men raping women, it never ends. Chivalry is dead. Women aren't objects, it really pisses me off."

"You're one of the good guys, Henry. Always quiet, always polite."

I was hoping she would ask if I'd like to watch her eat her sandwich. Please ask me that Jasmine.

"I try Jasmine, I try. Can I ask you a question?"

"Of course, what's up?"

"They are doing a small showing of the 1957 short film The Red Balloon at Montgomery theater this Friday, I'm just curious if you would be available to accompany me?"

"Oh..."

I snap out of my daydream and take a sip of the lukewarm Harpoon. Grab a Marlboro, tap it on my thumbnail and put it between my lips and light it, the wisp of smoke trying in vain to obscure my rapidly forming sneer.

I rise from the sofa and walk into the bedroom. Black curtains and black bedding. I like it dark in here. It's calming to me, light is similar to Barry and soccer mom whore, they're all intrusions to me. Muting them is about self-preservation. The neighborhood is safer when the quiet envelops me, I can appear normal with a steady dose of solitude.

I step over to the closet and slide the doors open. I reach down and unlock the padlock on my wooden chest. I spent two years building this beautifully lacquered work of art. A labor of love. I reach down and grab The Suns hair and yank her out of her home. Unlock the handcuffs, cut the duct tape from her mouth and lead her to the dining room.

"You sick mother fucker, you ugly, psycho mother fucker" she screams.

Hair all tangled, snot running down her nose, eyes full of rage and terror. I couldn't hide my smile. I briefly considered cutting her tongue out a week ago, she loves to throw "mother fuckers" around but they grew on me. They were almost tender names now, I craved them. I depended on them.

I put her dinner on a piece of white china and placed it in front of her. Put a cold Budweiser on the table next to the plate and gave her a cloth napkin.

"Drink your beer, Sun. I finally obtained a copy of The Red Balloon on DVD today, so after I watch you eat that tuna sandwich, we'll cuddle up and enjoy a great movie together. Does that sound good to you, Jasmine?"

Her slender fingers lightly gripped the bread.

About the Author:

Chris Milam lives in Hamilton, Ohio. He's a voracious reader and a diehard Washington National fan. He rarely strays far from his coffee cup or his beloved couch.

Fresh Paint
Arwen Faulkner

It was over.

In the pre-dawn darkness, alone with her thoughts, she let the knowledge settle over her soul. Into her bones. And she wondered, not for the first time, how it came to be that two people who had once loved each other so fiercely could become little more than strangers passing in the night. Maybe they'd never really known one another at all. Perhaps they'd lived in that Lover's Illusion of Fate and Destiny for so long, they'd begun to believe its authenticity, to believe in its fairy-tale ending. When in reality, a lover's vision sees only what it wants to see, and nothing more. The truth could remain hidden for decades. Lovers know only what they wish to know. See only what they wish to see.

And he couldn't see her.

He couldn't see how hard she had tried to be what he wanted. How she had struggled to make him happy, to give him whatever it was he insisted mattered most. She had sacrificed her own desires until it hurt. But still, he felt no loyalty towards her. He mocked her to others. Belittled her behind closed doors. Made her feel so small, it was as though the carbon inside her body had turned to diamond. It cut away at her heart until there was almost nothing left.

They used to argue passionately—yelling, screaming and boldly accusing—until they ran out of steam. Then they'd come together, the weight of their bodies crushing any doubts, confident that they belonged to each other. But she didn't want him to touch her anymore. In fact, she was grateful for the nights he fell asleep early, and didn't ask. There were more and more of those nights recently.

She lit a cigarette, and stared past the frosted window to a house across the street. Red and green Christmas lights blinked on-and-off. On-and-off. In the quiet glow of early-morning, she took off her armour, once and for all, and made the decision not to fight anymore.

*

"I want a divorce," she said.

Plain and straight, no sharp edges, no harsh undertones. Just like that. And she knew instantly that it was true. Oh, sure, she'd said it in not-so-many words before. Maybe even exactly those words. But this time was different. This time, she meant it.

"I want a divorce, David," she repeated. In case he hadn't heard her clearly, or even at all. She could recall countless occasions in the past when he'd tuned her out.

He sat on the couch in front of her, staring blankly at the TV screen, pretending—or perhaps, actually succeeding— to watch the hockey game. He didn't look over, didn't so much as cast a glance in her direction. Refused to meet her eyes, or acknowledge that she had, in fact, spoken out loud. To him.

In the old days, it wouldn't have mattered. She'd have sighed, stormed off, and things would have eventually cooled off. Gone back to normal; they always did. But something inside her had changed over the past few months. She no longer craved the comfort that accompanied the conscious decision to sweep everything under the rug. She no longer found peace in pretending to be happy when she wasn't, or trying to make nice with someone who refused to reciprocate. In the end, she was faced with one decision: stay and die a slow, painful death of the soul—or leave.

Not really a choice at all. It was time to start over, that much was certain. A lifetime of running away had taught her to be sure before she left—one hundred percent positive. Convinced there was no other way. And she was. It was ridiculous to think she'd wasted five years on this relationship. It seemed silly to call it a marriage, really, when the term itself implied two forces entwining and melding to become one greater than either individually—their relationship had been anything but.

Instead of discussion, there were demands. Instead of understanding, there was condescension. Instead of Quality Time, there was time in front of the TV, eyes ahead, no conversation. Instead of honesty and truth-telling, there was manipulation. Betrayal. A deep-rooted lack of trust—from both sides—that pervaded everything. There was no "talking it out and working it through." They were on separate teams, fighting opposing battles, for entirely different reasons. It was exhausting.

"I'm going to start looking for a place tomorrow. I don't really see the point in waiting. We both know nothing's going to change." She cleared her throat. "David, are you listening to me?" He stared straight ahead. *And the beat goes on.*

Looking around at the accumulation of years, she imagined cardboard boxes with permanent marker labels all lined up in a row by the door, and suitcases filled with clothes, toys, and other things you just can't live without. She pictured the kitchen appliances all boxed up, hidden behind packing tape, and ready to go. She could almost smell the fresh paint on her new apartment walls, and felt a rush of sheer excitement knowing the future would unwrap itself like a gift, one box at a time. Freedom. That's what fresh paint smelled like.

The images faded. She sighed, and shifted her weight, extremely conscious of the fact he had yet to reply. A scorching heat rose up from her belly, climbed her esophagus, and threatened to choke her. "David?"
Silence. The lights from the television flickered in his eyes—nothing more. She turned on her heels and slowly walked away. Down the long hall, past the children, sound asleep, into the office. Closing the door, she sat down hard in the black leather chair, and put her head in her hands. Then she cried, a good long cry, until she could cry no more.

About the Author:
Arwen Faulkner currently resides in Ottawa, ON where she divides her time between being a wife and mom-of-four, a student at Carleton University, and director of *The Journal Project* (www.journalproject.net). Arwen hopes to inspire others to follow their dreams. Books are her best friends. Fear is her worst enemy. Poetry and ice-cream are her weaknesses. Writing has always been her saving grace.

The Green Datsun
Helen Bar-Lev

"I'm going to have an accident", I said to my husband on my 29th birthday, "with the car"... The children were two and three years old, playing sweetly in the other room. "Being dramatic as usual; sometimes I think you're crazy" Newman scoffed. A favorite expression. He was thirty. A thirty-year-old believes life is forever, even if he's majoring in psychology. A bald, muscular psychology major. We were living then in Los Angeles , in a middle-class modest neighborhood of identical pre-fab, two bedroom houses, each with a magnolia tree in front near the curb. The houses had attached garages, all of which had been illegally converted into an extra room. This is what a student-couple could afford and would do for the time-being. On the front lawn stood a tall and broad mulberry tree which painted the driveway burgundy in late spring and shed its fruit faster than anyone could pick them. In the back yard grew a prolific apricot tree, hollyhocks, a vegetable garden and a large weeping willow under which the children would sit stuffing themselves with the delicious apricots during the month of June.

That premonition began just after my last birthday when Newman bought me a Datsun, pastel green, small, four doors. I didn't particularly fancy that hue of green, which Nature also did not find pleasing enough to use in its palette. But it didn't clash with trees or grass like some greens do. In fact, it was such an unobtrusive color that it sometimes seemed invisible, especially when I was trying to locate it in a parking lot or even on the street. Always the individualist, it eventually dawned on me that this distinctive color made my car unique and therefore more endearing. Besides, it drove like a sports car, smooth as butter, instantly responsive. Never mind that it looked like a box. Actually the color was similar to that of pistachio ice cream. I was petite, it was also; a perfect match between human and car. I came to love it.

Newman drove a turquoise Volkswagen Beetle to and from work and studies. Everyone then drove VW Beetles. One day I drove it in a Santa Ana wind storm and it blew into the adjacent lane of the freeway, which was, by great fortune, unoccupied at that moment. That incident and its pedals which were difficult to press down, had prompted the gift of the Datsun.

Months went by. The premonition did not leave, but I didn't mention it again. One December day we took a drive in the Datsun to the hills north of Los Angeles to show the children the snow - and hit a deer who had jumped out from the woods at a 45 degree angle to the car. A large and elegant creature, it lay motionless by the side of the road; we thought it was dead. Newman got out of the car and approached it. As he did so, the deer sprung up and leapt away. "There's your accident" he said, mocking again. So. He hadn't forgotten. But I knew it wasn't. Definitely not. Sometimes I really despised him (especially now for hitting the deer), but put those feelings out of conscious reach into my mental file of unfinished business, to be dealt with when University was done and the children a bit older. Little Annie and Allen, sleeping in the back, were unaware.

It was ten p.m. Spring again. The fragrance of citrus blossoms wafted through the cool air. There was an almost-full moon and the feeling was delicious. I had just finished a night course in Anthropology at UCLA and was driving home, a pleasant, fifteen-minute drive, quiet at that time of night. I was excited by that evening's lesson and alert. Ahead, where the road rose slightly and then sloped back down again, railroad tracks crossed. No gates, no warning signals, probably not in use for a long time.

I began to turn left – and then it happened – a car coming opposite and speeding like a rocket smashed into the right rear door of the Datsun. I did not see it coming, just felt the impact and the car spinning round and round in circles, with the most absurd feeling of relief. *Finally*! And strangely, almost surrealistically, two men fled the other car and disappeared into a vacant lot that was conveniently available to them.

I rested my head on the steering wheel, exhausted from the months of waiting for this, not that I had foreseen *how* it would happen, just that it was inevitable... "Are you all right, should we phone an ambulance?" Two Goliath policemen loomed over me, pretending to be friendly. "No, I'm okay". They muttered something about the "damn blind spot" and all the accidents that had happened here, then asked where the other car's occupants had gone. I pointed to the bushes. In a dash they were off, heavy boots lifted off the ground with the agility of ballerinas. Strange I had never known about the blind spot... When they returned with the two culprits, handcuffed, one of the policemen came back. "That car is stolen. If this gets to court and you have to testify, say they threatened you with this knife", and he held out a hunting knife. "But they didn't", I said in my young-mother innocence. "Well, you just say they did, understand?" But no more was heard of the incident.

How odd that the premonitions persisted. Sometimes one side of me would have a conversation with the other, trying to convince me to get in the car and drive, while the other side would forbid it. Most often I could reason with it or ignore it.

Next year. 1971. February. The earthquake occurred at six in the morning. We were sleeping when the house began to vibrate. The closet door in the bedroom, which was a slatted, folding one, had been rigged by Newman to activate the electricity inside when opened. Now it was banging open-shut-open-shut, light-dark-light-dark, until the electricity was cut and only the door continued to bang wildly, as though a mad goblin was behind it all. In his panic, Newman's arms clamped around me as I was struggling to get out of bed to reach the children, whose bedroom was on the other side of ours. Was he asleep? He was a big man, strong, muscular, an antithesis to my thinness. "The children", I cried, freeing myself, but the shaking was so severe that I kept falling. Dishes were smashing, bookcases crashing. Wild and thundering noises were coming from everywhere. Allen, who always awoke crying, slept fastly. Annie, who always slept late and woke serenely, was awake and crying. I reached them, calmed them, then the earth stopped shaking.

During the day we listened intently to the news, cleaned up the broken dishes, lifted fallen book-shelves, securing them to the wall with big bolts. The dam was holding, but if not, we'd have to leave. That night I surprised myself by awakening to my own screams. I had not realized, during the daytime, how terrified I was. The aftershocks, frequent and severe, continued throughout the long night, like a ship hitting stormy waves.

The next day electricity still had not been restored. People had been killed. The university's library was in shambles, the windows all broken, books scattered. Not one bookcase remained standing, there, where Newman sat for many hours each weekday. We did not leave the house. The mulberry tree had fallen on the Datsun, wrecking it.

And finally, as though the Datsun, the accident, had been a dream and the earthquake had finally shaken me awake, the premonitions stopped and never returned.

About the Author:

Helen Bar-Lev was born in New York in 1942 (www.helenbarlev.com). She has lived in Israel for 42 years and has held over 90 exhibitions of her landscape paintings. Her poems and artwork have appeared in numerous online and print anthologies. Helen is Assistant to the President of Voices Israel www.voicesisrael.com and Senior Editor of Cyclamens and Swords Publishing.

An Unusual Day at the Met
Richard Kyllonen

I arrived at the Metropolitan Museum of Art on Saturday around noon. It was my first visit to the museum and I planned on walking haphazard through the galleries to observe whatever attractions caught my eye. It would turn out to be much more memorable than that.

Not long after I arrived, I encountered Lindsey Lohan in Charles Engelhard Court. The sun shined through the windows and cast checkerboards of light upon the walls and floor. We were both admiring a sculpture by Hermon Atkins MacNeil called *The Sun Vow*, depicting a boy aiming a bow at the sky while standing closely to a seated chieftain. Lindsay looked quite demure in a gray peplum dress as she took notes in a black marble composition notebook. I became a little star-struck while staring at Lindsay, appreciating a more natural beauty than is apparent on the magazine covers. She glanced in my direction and I quickly turned away. She noticed.

"I am fascinated by images of the rites of passage," she remarked with a smile. "I envision this young Sioux becoming a warrior as his arrow pierces the sun."

I was almost as surprised by her insightful observation as I was by the fact that she acknowledged me. I struggled to respond.

"I like bronze sculptures," I said.

"As do I," she said with a chuckle. "Although I am more passionate about Greek terracotta figurines and the marble sculptures of Bernini."

"Oh yes, Bernini," I replied. "I like him." I had no idea who Bernini was.

Lindsay went on in great detail about the tragedy of lost love represented in Bernini's *Apollo and Daphne*. She had a way of letting her conversation drift along tangents, and somehow Bernini turned into Michelangelo, Greek literature, the Pythagorean Theorem and the irrational nature of the square root of two. She was a plethora of knowledge.

The monologue drew to a close and Lindsay suggested we make our way to the galleries for Ancient Near Eastern Art. "The palatial art is amazing, with all the intricate engravings. I have studied the Assyrian Empire quite extensively, and my song *Bossy* was heavily influenced by the life of Queen Semiramis, the first queen of Assyria."

Lindsay led the way as we ventured to a gallery depicting the Assyrian Royal Court. It was obvious that she frequented the museum often, as she didn't need to refer to a visitor's map or any such resource. Lindsay put her hand on my shoulder and said "you must see this" as we stopped before a figure of a winged bull and winged lion with a human head. "Isn't it wonderful?"

I nodded with vague interest when Lindsay suddenly shouted across the gallery. "Justin! Hey, over here!"

I turned my head and was shocked to see Justin Bieber walking towards us. Mr. *Baby, baby, baby* himself. He was comfortably adorned in a red sweater vest with tan Dockers and a baseball cap. Justin and Lindsay hugged and traded pleasantries. "Justin, I'd like you to meet … umm, I'm sorry, I didn't catch your name."

"It's Rich," I said.

Justin shook my hand and said "It's such a great pleasure to meet you, Rich. There is nothing I like better than to meet new friends who appreciate fine art. Music is a trivial pursuit when compared to the knowledge that can be absorbed in museums such as this."

"I was just showing, umm, Rich, this great Mesopotamian work," Lindsay said.

"Oh, yes," Justin replied. "A fine example of the utilization of gypsum alabaster to achieve intricate detail."

We strolled down the room and Justin appeared to be reading from the wall. "Let us celebrate with the people of all the lands in peace and happiness." All I saw was a progression of wedge-shaped symbols.

"Where do you see that?" I asked.

Justin pointed to the cryptic shapes and replied, "Right there."

"Justin is very busy touring and recording," Lindsay interjected, "but he spends his free time studying cuneiform, a writing style used by many ancient civilizations. He has become quite proficient."

We spent several hours admiring ivory, stone and metal pieces of art from various kingdoms. Lindsay made notations in her notebook while Justin texted observations to his friends. Finally, Justin said, "I've been here all day. What do you guys think, why don't we go out and party?"

OK, I thought to myself, *here we go. Jane Ballroom, the Boom Boom Room, the Darby. All the hotspots. I'll get to see how the celebrities let loose.*

"I'm feeling a little wild tonight," Lindsay said. "Let's go crazy."

"I know how you feel, girl. I have just the place," Justin answered.

They looked into each other's eyes and exclaimed, "Coney Island!"

We made our way out of the museum and were swarmed by photographers and followers of the two megastars. Justin and Lindsay stood outside the doors and spent 20 minutes signing autographs for all their adoring fans. Justin signed his hat and presented it to a young boy in a wheelchair who was wearing a shirt stating *I'm a Belieber.* When all the fans were satisfied, Justin and Lindsay posed for the photographers.

"These paparazzi are so crazy," Justin said.

"I know," replied Lindsay. "What great people."

The paparazzi graciously let us through when the pictures were done and we made our way to Justin's black Ford Fusion, parked along the road four blocks away. "Oops," he said. "It looks like the parking meter has expired." He fished through his pocket, pulled out several quarters and fed them into the meter. "There, that should cover it." He unlocked the car doors and remarked, "This car is so fuel-efficient and environmentally friendly. Definitely my kind of vehicle."

Justin punched our destination into the GPS and plugged his iPad into the car's USB port. I expected a medley of *Bieber's Greatest Hits*, but instead, the brilliant voice of Pavarotti performing *Nessun Dorma* exploded from the speakers. The music transitioned to several pieces from Mozart's *Requiem.* Lindsay was mesmerized, barely speaking a word, and Justin waved an imaginary conductor's baton with his right hand.

I was impressed with the way Justin used his turn signals and yielded to pedestrians in the crosswalks as we made our way to Brooklyn. At one point, Justin shook his head and said "Gosh darn, I wasn't paying attention. I think I was exceeding the speed limit by four or five miles per hour. I hate when that happens."

We arrived in Coney Island and parked the car. Justin had a little problem parallel parking and tapped the car in front of him, leaving a scratch on the rear bumper. He exited the car and grimaced upon assessing the damage. He returned to the Fusion and pulled out an envelope and a promotional picture from the glove compartment. He stuffed $1000 in the envelope, signed the picture "Sorry Dude. Love ya, The Biebs," and placed it under one of the car's wiper blades.

Lindsay and I had a great time on the extreme thrill rides. Sharp turns and dramatic drops on the Cyclone. A 90 mph ascent on the Sling Shot and then a freefall. Somersaults in the air while swinging at high speeds on Zenobio. Lindsay was rather reserved, though at one point she did exclaim, "This is so scary." I screamed like a maniac and nearly cried.

Justin shied away from the high speed rides. I think his stomach was bothering him. He ventured to the mild ride section and had fun on the Happy Swing and the Big Top Express, a circus themed train. He was a little bothered by the Mermaid Parade, a mini log flume, because he had given away his hat and ended up getting his hair wet. The Whac-A-Mole game was his favorite.

Lindsay and I hooked up with Justin when we were done with the rides. It had been a long day and we were tired, but Lindsay had an idea. "I know the perfect way to end the evening," she proclaimed.

She and Justin shared a grin and shouted in unison, "Cotton candy!"

We purchased the billowy treat at a stand and enjoyed it seated upon a wooden bench. Then, alas, it was time to go. They were kind enough to pose with me for a few pictures on my iPhone before we parted ways. Justin gave me $500 for a taxi to get me wherever I needed to go, asking me, as he placed the bills in my hand, "Do you think that's enough?"

What started out as a simple visit to the Met turned into a day spent with two of the most well-known celebrities in the world. As I walked away, they were making plans to get a good night's sleep and meet at the New York City Library the next morning to read passages from Walt Whitman's "Leaves of Grass." They were anxious to discuss the poetry, its symbolism and the celebration of nature. Two free spirits looking to expand their minds while pursuing good, clean fun. What a wonderful experience.

About the Author:

Richard Kyllonen graduated from Heidelberg University in Tiffin, Ohio with a degree in English and Psychology. After a stellar career in the CIA as an undercover agent in the international anti-terrorism division, Richard transitioned to a life as a freelance rodeo clown. He currently enjoys writing short stories and teaching advanced martial arts as a Taekwondo Grandmaster.

FLASH FICTION

Stepping in Shit
Alex Casola

You walk into the room and I can tell by the look on your face that we're going to have it out. You have that scowl that means you stepped in dog shit again and it's my fault because I'm too lazy to clean it up. I don't dare look down from your face in case you're holding your shoe in your hand. I don't want you to know that I have any clue that I've done something wrong.

Thankfully, you haven't stepped in Chile's shit. You just had to get out of your car to move the trashcans up the driveway. The same trashcans that you had to take out last night. And you ask me, or rather interrogate me, have I even left the house today, or did I just not see the trashcans? You're turning red by the time you get to the part where you don't know which one is worse.

"I took Chile for a run," I lie. Really all I did was open the door for him when he cried to go out and stood in the doorway waiting for him to do his thing, pulling my robe shut closer against the winter weather. Chile's shit steamed in the frozen grass of our small yard.

You roll your eyes. Either your eye-roll has gotten more exaggerated from having to do it so often or you want me to know that you know that I'm full of shit. "How many jobs did you apply for today?"

"Three," I lie again.

"I just don't know why you're not getting any calls back." You're breaking down, feeling sorry for me, hoping that you haven't wasted so much money paying the rent for two with a false belief in me.

"Just a bad economy." And for emphasis I run my hands through my greasy hair and give you a stricken look that says, I hate this too.

"I just can't stand to see you rot here."

"I'm fine really."

"No, you're not." It's the first time you admit this, at least to me. I ask you what you want to do for dinner to change the subject even though it points out that I haven't planned or prepared anything. Maybe you won't notice.

About the Author:
Alex Casola is a short story writer living in Denver Colorado. She has a Bachelor of Arts Degree in English from the University of Florida. Her stories, "The Recycled Apartment," and "Wisdom Teeth," have appeared in the undergraduate magazine, *The Mangrove Review.*

The Electric Typewriter
Greg McKenzie

About a month ago, I bought a typewriter off a guy on Craigslist. I thought it would get me excited about writing again.

We agreed on fifty bucks for it.

I hopped on the streetcar once I got home from work, went ten minutes down the track, then hopped off at Euclid street, walked five minutes up.

I hit the bell, and he answered quickly. He had the box out, opened it up, plugged it in, showed me that it worked.

"The ink ribbon is pretty fresh, so it should last you," he said. He had a gay accent. "It's been sitting in this box, in my parents garage forever, never really needed it," he said.

"Perfect," I said, gave him a fifty, put it in the box, walked it to the streetcar stop and brought it home.

The box said "QUIET TYPING" in big, flashy, italic letters. That's why I bought that one -- I didn't want to be a burden on my roommates. I had seven of them.

I brought it upstairs and plugged it in, fed a fresh piece of paper through it and hit the keyboard.

THWACK... THWACK... I could hear the damn keys reverberating off the walls. I left a water bottle on the electric keyboard and let it ring out, while I stepped outside my door to see how loud it really was.

It was loud.

I thought I'd better save the typing for during the day, or I'd get shit from seven directions. Night time is when the good ideas came. Thoughts are cleaner somehow.

I typed during the day a couple days a week. I'd drink wine right when I got in the door after work to get in the mood. I pumped out three crappy pieces, then the ink ribbon wore out. Now, it just punches little dimples into the paper.

It's sitting right next to me, and I don't know whether or not I should sell it on Craigslist. I could use the fifty, forty bucks -- whatever I can get for it. It just needs a new ribbon.

I only the bought the damn thing because I thought it would get me excited about writing again. It's been sitting on the floor, next to my desk for over a month now.

I went to the shit Chinese mall today and bought a new keyboard. Sort of an old one with big wobbly keys that clack quietly when you type. I like writing on it. I'm writing at night, regularly. I hope it lasts.

About the Author:
Greg McKenzie lives, works, writes and plays music primarily out of Toronto. He is twenty five years old.

Sometimes Sandy
Cheryl Anne Gardner

Sandy's sad all the time. Sad for no good reason. Punch my fist through the back of her head sad and miserable. All the time. Except when she listens to the radio. She does like to listen to the radio. That's how we met. Over an antique transistor radio. She says it calms her down when she can imagine herself inside the songs, inside even the bad ones. The reds change to blues and the electric whites in her eyes to infinite grays just knowing that in roughly three minutes the story will be over. She says she likes the idea of being over. She's tried. It's not that simple. Me, I want to disappear, slowly, from knowing her. She smiles and then licks her food. And my food. And then she turns to scout out anyone else's food left unattended. It's embarrassing. She chews her nails and dresses for shit too, like an anime schoolgirl sat eating scabs in a fine restaurant next to a giant dung beetle in a billycock and six-fold. I'm the beetle. I try not to look across the table at her. All the food and the booze and the chintz covered walls closing in on her are making her sweat, and she is making me sweat, so I tell her I'm a sailor, then I make a noose from the cooking twine in my pocket so I can pull the half-chewed food out of her throat when she starts choking like she always does in public. Knock. Knock. Who's there? Sandy. Fidgety, sweaty, crazy-eyed Sandy. Or maybe it's the pepper sauce.

"Are you ok?" I ask, but she just shoves a fistful of knuckle into her mouth, so I say it again: "Sandy? Are you ok?"

She thinks there are too many people. In the room. In the world. "It's a Tuesday night. I'm ok, but why are there so many people? That man's elbow is literally in my plate. Do you think they know how crowded it is? The management? It feels crowded, don't you think."

I don't know, and I don't care. What difference does it make that it's Tuesday? She doesn't even know these people. "Can you please just--" I stop myself before I say what I want to say. The waiter fills my wine glass. He's smirking.

Twice Sandy and I had the antibiotic-injected steak and the bitter-almond torte here. Today it's radioactive squid and Vietnamese coffee jelly. Sandy smells like a meadow. The taxi driver has a picture of one on his visor. Old Country. That's my memory of her now, in this moment: a yellow taxi, billowing exhaust fumes on a hill in a Romanian meadow. I stand in the kitchen, feet cold against the tile. Her voice echoes up the staircase, crushes my lungs when I inhale it over the vodka martini in my hand. I'm afraid of what might happen to us if I leave. If I manage somehow to control the twisting and the spinning left without balance, will there still be a Sandy? Will there still be a me? What if? What if she's not lying next to me, drunk, cowering under the covers at three in the morning, will I still want to punch her over the ignorance, the uneaten squid . . . and all those bags of vomit she tries to hide in the basement? Tries to hide from me.

About the Author:

When she isn't writing, Cheryl Anne Gardner likes to chase marbles on a glass floor, eat lint, play with sharp objects, and make taxidermy dioramas with dead flies. She writes art-house novellas and abstract flash fiction, some published, some not.

FEATURED POET

DARREN M. EDWARDS is a performance poet, essayist and teacher. He received both his B.S. and his M.S. in English from Utah State University. After graduating, he started his own publication project, *New Graffiti: Literature on the Streets,* which received a "Best in State" award from *City Weekly*. His essays and poetry have appeared in a number of journals including *The Southern Quill, Referential Magazine, Camas*, and *Stone Voices*.

.

Witness
Darren M. Edwards

You can hear her screaming
from the other side of the room
wide eyed
tight toothed
close lipped
silent.
She's got this one bulbous
knuckle like all the pent up screams
have pitched camp in the joint
at the middle of her middle finger.

Her three-year-old is pulling
at the hem of her pants crying
Mommy, momma, mom, mom, mommy
and I can see it in the way
her cheek rises at the corner
like it's trying to pinch a single sheet
of paper to her eye—She might lose it.
But the trick is
the paper being pinched
between her cheek
and that eye
is scrawled all over with marching orders
for those rising screams.

But her three-year-old is crying
Mommy, momma, mom, mom, mommy

And, the nurse is fumbling through files.
And, the overgrown mustache sitting next to her
is eyeing the line of her denims as they round her hip.
And, the middle aged gaggle across the room is whispering,
not so quietly, about her inattention to the child.
And, I'm fiddling with my glasses
like a scientist watching the slow traverse of stars.

And her three-year-old is crying
Mommy, momma, mom, mom, mommy.

So, when she stands
sudden,
unannounced,
three-year-old attached at the hem,
everything stops.

I can feel my shoulders tighten
as she lifts the child onto her hip,
takes three brisk strides to the nurse,
child now pulling at her blouse,
her mouth opens,
                    and the gaggle is holding their breath
                    and their whispers.
          Even the mustache has traded his leer
          for a look of quizzical concern,
and I'm waiting for a supernova,
some cosmic collision,
another big bang
when she asks
in the most polite tone
how much longer might the wait be?
And, the nurse smiles
gesturing with the space between two fingers
just a little while longer.

Lowering the child to the floor
she retakes her seat,
where she can feel the whispers
and the eyes,
and she goes back to rubbing her thumb
in circles over that knuckle,
circle after
circle
to the rhythm of all those screams
marching on.

I'm Not Yet Ready
Darren M. Edwards

Sitting at the desk in my office,
I watched a dark chocolate brown
spider scratching its way across
the wall just above my window.

It came to me at that moment
the sudden flash of revelation
the deft imprint of knowing
when I will be ready for heaven.

It has nothing to do with sheltering
the poor or feeding the hungry,
there is no number of babies
I can save from burning buildings,
or amount of blistered, cracked and bloodied
toes from long desert pilgrimages
that will open that great gate.
Stitching my lips closed with a vow of silence,
starving myself until the bend of my belly has turned inward,
castration, flagellation, revelation, religious participation,
and mummification would all serve me to no avail.

No, the day I'll be ready for heaven
the day I will ride up into the sky on an
escalator of glass with silver streamers
and those little glittery sparkly squares
they use to decorate high school dances,
and angels like Dino and Frank will
welcome me home in a chorus of
Ain't That a Kick in the Head?
that day,
that glorious gold trimmed
Mother Teresa resting on a futon day
that fresh and clean like the Downy bear day,

that will be the day
my eyes scroll along the wall
above my window
and I let the little
eight legged bastard
live.

Reconstructing Pandora
Darren M. Edwards

In high school
I made a green ceramic box
with a little man peaking out.
His big blue marbles of eyes
just pushing the top of the box open,
but these eyes
they weren't just marbles.
They were the rainbow striped slammer
every kid on the block wanted,

they were the dice in the sweat slicked hand
of every praying gambler from the back allies
to the Rio,

they were the pearl earrings
carried across the ocean
in the pocket of a pregnant Scottish woman
so she could pass them on to her only daughter—
her first child to be born in the land of hope,

they were the headlights on my grandfathers
Chrysler
the one he used as a down payment on the house
one-thousand-eight-hundred and sixty-seven-miles
away from his parents
and everything he'd ever known
the house he'd raise his daughters in
and one day sitting at the kitchen table
crack jokes with his grandson

they were the eyes of Ken Brewer
watching the Bear River
snake under a weather worn
wood fence as he realized that,
"a fence never kept the moon out
of the rye"

they were the eyes I slyly shifted
two seats to the left
in that high school ceramics class
to check out the girl with short brown hair
and the face that made me want to swallow
a whole block of clay
just to slow the rise and fall of my chest,

they are the eyes of every child to young
to grasp mortality standing at the edge
of a sealed box being lowered into a grave,

and the eyes of the parents without words
standing next to them,

and in that box, and behind these eyes
lay the same thing
and for all our wired connections,
freeways,
earthquake proof skyscrapers
looking over fields where
the dust of our civilization
weighs heavy with the blood of young men,

for our laws
and supreme court breakthroughs
for the walls we've constructed to support
and contain our world
for all of this
we have nothing more
than what we started with
behind those eyes and in that box.

The Competition
Darren M. Edwards

Our mother cringes,
gripping the wheel tighter
with each round
of this sibling competition;
though, it really is more
a battle of the sexes
where our most awkward
frailties and bodily functions
form the front line fodder.

Sitting in the back seat of our
old Wagoner my sister whispers
Panties in a poisonous tone,
which I casually parry with
an enthusiastic *Jockstrap*.

An evil grin spreading across
her face she blurts *PMS*
and I retort, in a squeaky yet
proud voice, *testicles*.

Hiding her revulsion
at the thought of the
wrinkled little oysters
she manages, *Ovaries*!

But, quick thinking allows me
to use *Pubes* before she does;
since, technically it could
go either way.

Realizing I had dealt her
a double blow, she reaches deep
into her bag of icky femininity
to hit me with *Tampon*.

My nine-year-old mind
momentarily stunned,
frozen there picturing
all the things I wished I
hadn't seen while passing the
garbage can in our shared bathroom,
it takes me longer than I'd like
to stutter out the single syllable,
Sp-Sperm.

Rounds pass in a blur as we burn
through: *boner, uterus, scrotum,*
douche, condom, queef, wet dream,
fallopian tubes, foreskin,
and *labia*—though I had no idea what the
last one was.

Rounding the final turn home
our mother sighs, knowing the game
will soon be over.

In a final effort to seal my victory
I try to steal *Urethra* but the bump of
the driveway jars me before I can
get the word out.

Night Watch

(For Graham, Aidan, Alex and Jonah)

Darren M. Edwards

The grass is wet from the sprinklers at the old baseball field,
where an orange glow reaches from the moon lighting our way.
Looking at the stars, I feel the grasp of fingers, still sticky
from an ice cream sundae, pull at my pinky.
How many stars are there? My nephew asks,
his eyes still stuck up in the sky. *Always one more than you think.*
I answer, lifting him on my shoulders.
If we climb that hill do you think we could touch one?
His voice, wrapped in the evening breeze,
carries the short distance to my ears.
I don't tell him the stars are billions of miles away,
there's no point in having a discussion of time and space
with a three year old. *I suppose we ought to try huh?*
His arms tighten around my neck as we climb the hill.
The journey holds disappointment – we cannot touch the stars.
I prepare my explanation, some fluff about not giving up and Neil Armstrong.
When quietly, breathing behind my ear, he whispers, *Maybe we should jump?*

Motivation:

I write poetry for the same reason I write fiction and creative nonfiction, there is an itch in my mind and it needs to be scratched. There is an idea which is not yet fully formed, and it's crying to be finished. There is an issue or problem that I need to try and make sense of. That, and the fact that it's adorable watching my dog give me a confused look as I read my work out loud while revising it or polishing the performance of a finished piece.

FEATURED ARTIST

Stephen Algera has been an artist and illustrator based out of Hamilton for over ten years. His work is influenced by many different artists and mediums, ranging from traditional illustration, print making, etching, comic books and graphic novels, surrealism, and Japanese prints. His favourite artists are Hokusai, Arthur Rackham, Gustave Doré, Edward Gorey, Albrecht Durer, Alphonse Mucha, Andy Warhol, Kevin Eastman, Peter Laird, Geoff Darrow, and Matt Groening. "As a whole, my work encompasses a juxtaposition of the ancient and the modern. The purpose of my work is to illustrate ancient and modern principles, not as a criticism, but just to mirror these ideas to society; to invite people to see the same things that I see; encourage discussion and draw conclusions they may have never considered before."

"Hello Kamikaze"
Mixed media on paper, 8 X 10 inches (2011)

"Nothing's Sacred"
Mixed media on paper, 11 X 17 inches (2008)

"Irish Rover"
Mixed media on paper, 8 X 10 inches (2012)

"Le Kangarou Boxeur"
Mixed media on paper, 8 X 10 inches (2012)

"Koi"
Acrylic on canvas board, 8 X 12 inches (2008)

About the Artist:

In 2005, Stephen Algera graduated from the McMaster University Visual Arts program which was held at the Dundas Valley School of Art. Since then, he has seen his work appear in various galleries and art shows across the greater Hamilton and Toronto areas such as the Blue Angel, Arcadia, the Artword Artbar galleries, This Ain't Hollywood, Lister Arts, and the Fakture gallery, which is based out in Denver, Colorado. In addition, he's participated in yearly art auctions for the Dundas Valley School of Art and for an online art auction hosted by Curry's art supplies boutique, in which proceedings went for research purposes at the Dystonia Medical Research Foundation of Canada.

About Zombies:

People like zombie movies because they are zombies. Have a look at any city street and you'll see these brain dead monsters everywhere. They're all talking to themselves standing on street corners, eating hotdogs, pushing strollers diddling cell phones. They're all tweeting and texting and updating their statuses muttering the same crazy shit to each other, "like, like, like."

~ Peter Jelen

www.ingramcontent.com/pod-product-compliance
Lightning Source LLC
Chambersburg PA
CBHW070353130626
46556CB00007B/3160